CREATIO

AMALGAMATION OF SHORT POEMS

VAIDEHI PUROHIT

to myself for ones

Contents

Foreword

The poems are a bit dark and deep. Many of the poems showcase pain and suffering of human life and the beauty of death. Reading the poems give a saddening view of the daily lives and how difficulty it is to survive in the human world

Preface

This book is an amalgamation of almost all the poems I have written since childhood . These poems are my way of expressing what I felt at that moment . Hence every single poem signifies different moments of my life .

Acknowledgements

I want to thank all the people I met in my life till now as every different experience inspired me to write something

Prologue

The book contains short poems based on struggles and difficulties of life which one makes in ones mind because of overthinking

POEMS

1. THUNDER

The sunlight fading away , whenever I wanted it to stay
Leaving the darkness behind
Which encapsulated me as I passed the time
The darkness is ominous
I feel it creeping inside me
Taking over my mind , body and soul
The night turns stormy with thunders aloud
As if they are telling me something through the cloud
I try to cover my ears but the thunder whispers
Something I could never understand
The reality desolving in the sand
As the rain starts with the thunder
I just stand there and shudder
It feels as if it's my death time now
As I look towards the sky and it growls
I stand there still waiting for the rain to drown me or for the thunder
to burn me alive
For my death,I strive
The thunder intensifies and so does the rain,as I feel all the pain
I feel relieved as I move towards death
But who knew it wasn't my last breath
I was still in the mortal world
But now I understood the thunders word
Death is what I wanted,but life is what I needed
Cause every time my wounds bleed,the darkness would strengthen

my creed

And the thunders whispers were Something I craved for peace .

• 4 •

2. AWRY

So many feelings unknown and lost
Feels like I am a ghost
Going crazy , but trying to be busy
To keep me sane
And endure all the pain
Cause this is the end .
Going astray, always a different way
Confused as hell ,
No , I am not well
Just want some peace
Just want one day
A silent place to stay
And a loving good night's kiss
To never wake up again .

3. LIFE

• 6 •

Sitting in one position,

Till eternity

Without any motion

It feels as if the world is crumbling down ,

With sadness in your heart you frown ,

People mumble beside you but you don't know what is true ,

You ask again and again and again but you can only feel pain , like

there are nails inserted in your heart , there is no end there was no

start , only pain , pain and pain .

4. DIFFICULTIES

Why just why ,I just have one question
Day after day in all my counselling sessions
The door closing on my face
Everyone leaving me outside
Feeling trapped in this whole world
Feeling caged in my own body
I have started loosing my breath
My only wish is death
All these responsibilities
All these expectations
All these eyes on me
Beyond them I am not able to see
Astray as eternity
I am just a fucking liability
Death is way better than living a life with several wounds in your soul
Living happily was never my goal
I just wanted to rest in peace
But now I am living like a lice
Sucking of of my parents
Giving them problems in return
I would rather like to be burned

5. CLUELESS

In a dark cave , you live your life
Never able to see the light
While challenges surrounding you
It is very hard to fight
Time goes by day after day
There was never a reason for you to stay
Day and night all are same
It is now impossible to distinguish
Everything is full of anguish
The damp and dark walls of the cave, starts to absorb you in them
slowly loosing your sanity
There was never any clarity
Death seems so peaceful now
But you are to unlucky you couldn't face it
And your surroundings you always blame it

6. FADING HOPE

The knot in my heart is loosening day by day

I am trying to find a way

There is a hope , there is a ray

That I would find a reason to stay ,

It's difficult, it's painful

But I want to my life to be peaceful

There would be many challenges through all the stages

The warm feeling that is present in my heart

Wasn't there from the start

The haze has started to clear

In my eyes there is a drop of tear

I want to cry ,but I need to try

My only wish is to silently die .

7. ALONE

Alone as eternity
Everyone of them left
I don't know what to do
I don't know where to go
Its just so difficult
I wanna die
I wanna cry
I just want to be at peace
All these thoughts, all these things are just eating me alive
Am i so bad
Am I nothing
All those days when we were smiling
You all are so easily forgetting
I just needed time ,
I didn't commit a serious crime
You are childish , you are immature
Its not my fault that you don't understand

8. FREEDOM

Wanna strangle myself to death
Wanna make it a painful last breath
Wanna induce so much pain ,its gonna be insane
And I won't dare complain
Would put a mask on my face
The wounds wouldn't leave a trace
I am so sick of all of this
Just need some quiet just need some peace .
Coz there is chaos inside
That I Wanna leave behind
But it just won't leave my side
But rather eat me alive
Slowly to my death , I strive

9. STRUGGLE

A mirage , an illusion
Which I make to keep myself going
It seems pretty believing
I am a master of betraying
Everyone but mostly myself
Just a drama without an end
Because the reality has desolved in sand
The feeling , the emotion , the expression on my face all are fake
Just waiting for someone to embrace
Every pain , every wound , every scar
Just need a safe space
To let me free

10. WOUNDS

Blood dripping from my soul
Wounds so deep inside
I just want them to hide
So confused , so lost
It's so painful , I don't know what
Just want to kill myself and bury deep in ground where there won't be
a single sound
I crave peace , I crave love
Just imagining a beautiful white dove
I have nothing to loose cause I beg for affection ,
While watching my own reflection
I just want to die a peaceful death ab feel cared for till my lats breath.

11. LIE

Sitting on a garden bench alone ,looking at a small flower
Contemplating what life is
Having hundreds of questions
Answering them with exclamations
Slowly fading away with time
I couldn't believe once I smiled
The flower seems so bright
It is hurting my eyes
There is no one to hear my cries
As the breeze blows
With the wind the flower flows
I feel so caged looking at it
I feel so raged as it goes away
And all I can do is stay
I don't have any option
This is my life's prophecy
I need to live my life in hypocrisy.

12. ASTRAY

The clouds covering the whole sky
Not leaving a single space
The Sunlight slowly fades
Wind making the trees tremble
Peacocks below the sky assemble
The rain starts gently
I open the window slightly
To feel the rain drops on my hand
It gives me the warmth I never had
The muddy smell gives me a homely feeling
But like others it would never be leaving
Enchanted by the heavenly rain
I happily endure the pain
The darkness of the clouds gives me peace
With the dark I wanna coalesce

13. ENCAPSULATION

Passing by trees
Passing by roads
Passing by so many different lives
Never waiting for anyone
Time can be ruthless
Time can be gracious
But it is just one of the illusions
Like all our situations
Travelling so far where Time doesn't exist
Where you are at peace
In the solitaire
You start to care
About those trees
About those roads
And the time you have left behind
there is no place to hide
The darkness is where now you reside.

14. NOTHINGNESS

Feeling so out of place
In this dark solace
Wanna cry so bad
But I am lying to myself
Wanna strangle myself
Wanna kill myself so bad
Fuck this world
Fuck these expectations
Fuck every fucking aspiration
Why torcher oneself
Why be so hard on yourself
Why struggle so much when you just have to die
Everything is just a big lie
There is no point of anything

15. CRAVING PEACE

The forest so dark and dusty
As if it has never been visited
Contains nothing yet everything to believe
There is no way in or no way out
You seem to fade away in it
In matter of an eyes blink
You don't know what to think
In this solitaire there is no time to spare
But there's gonna be no one who genuinely cares
Coz everyone is selfish
It's there fettish
Just standing still
You don't do nothing
It's hella scary
Everything is wary
You want answers
Beyond yourself
Just go to sleep forget everything
A sleep so deep You remember nothing

16. DEATH

Death , why is it so distinct
Why is it beyond our understanding
Why is it always negative
Why is it always bad
Why is it not good to be sad
I wanna die so damn much
I don't have any dream as such
I would also be okay just with a coma
Just wanna escape the real life trauma

17. STUPEFIED

I wanted to die

I wanted to lie

So deep below inside

I wanted to cry

I wanted to try

But there is no one with me beside , alone and solitaire

Who said life was fair

No one, there is no one who would really care

There is only so much I can bare

The thoughts and the pain tears me apart

There's no way my life would restart

Like a dried flower I am falling apart

As if the life was sucked out of me

I wish all of it was a dream

I want answers to all those questions

But there are none

Time moving leving me behind

It's too much for me all the daily grind

Please someone freeze my mind

End Note

THANK YOU TO ALL THE READERS